OUT OF DARKNESS

OUT OF DARKNESS

DIANE MOBLEY

ARPress
ILLUMINATING IDEAS
EMPOWERING VOICES

ARPress
45 Dan Road Suite 5
Canton MA 02021

Hotline: 1(888) 821-0229
Fax: 1(508) 545-7580

Ordering Information:
Quantity sales. Special discounts are available on quantity purchases by corporations, associations, and others. For details, contact the publisher at the address above.

Printed in the United States of America.

ISBN-13:   Softcover   979-8-89389-975-7
              eBook   979-8-89389-974-0

Library of Congress Control Number: 2024918454

TABLE OF CONTENTS

DIANE'S PAINTING

A few years after I started writing this book, I had a strong desire to paint a woman coming out of darkness. I didn't know it at the time, but the more I looked at the painting, the more I would see in the brush strokes. Everyone sees something different. The night I saw Michael as a little boy, my heart stopped. I knew this painting had special meaning.

DEDICATED TO

Ronnie Lee Mobley

A Wonderful Man, Husband and Father The Love of My Life

APPRECIATION

M y heartfelt thanks go to my family and Michael's friends, who did an interview with me and helped by contributing to this book. Some friends and family where unable to help, and my hope is that they find joy and peace again.

INTRODUCTION

"Out of Darkness" is the story of my son, Michael, and the grief we suffered due to our loss. Nothing can be more painful to a mother than to lose a child who is dearly loved.

Michael's passing had a huge impact on our family and friends. I could not accept that my precious son was gone. We all worked hard to move on, but nothing could stop the pain. Through the years my depression and guilt worsened until I was able to face the truth and receive my healing. Michael was dead and he took his own life.

When I first started writing this book, it was to help others with their pain, not fully understanding the healing it would bring for me and my family. Sharing the story of Michael has been the most effective therapy for us all. Now we can talk about him again and remember the good along with the bad. By sharing his story, we now have our joy and peace back. It has been a long journey. My hope is that it will help others to stop and think before making a decision to give up on life. *Tomorrow is a new day and where there is life, there is hope.*

CHAPTER 1

1994

I t is a typical Sunday morning. My husband Ronnie doesn't want me to go out alone in the middle of the night, so he rides with me while I throw my newspapers. My thoughts are of my twenty year old son, Michael, who from the time he walked into the house that night, had been acting strange.

I am worried about him, concerned that we left him brooding as he sat in a straight back chair in the corner of our darkened den. I know I hurt his feelings when I sarcastically asked him if he was feeling sorry for himself. I felt guilty as soon as I said it, but he had a way of making me feel guilty with that "poor me" look he put on so well.

I am confused and at wits end about what to do for him. How can I help him? We have tried so many things, but nothing seems to work. Michael keeps secrets. It is hard to figure him out. Ronnie and I aren't psychiatrists; we don't have the training to help him. We don't know what is going on in his life. We just don't trust him anymore. We love him so much. It is especially frustrating for me because Michael is my heart, my only son.

Around 4 AM I have the weirdest feeling that something is wrong at home. I begin to get agitated, upset, and panicky.

I wish I had insisted that Michael come with us on the route. I really didn't want to leave him. All of the sudden I blurt out,

"Ronnie, I need to stop and call Michael so I can check on him. There's something wrong at home; I just know it."

"Now honey, you know he's probably asleep, and you'll be done shortly. You can check on him when we get home."

I know that Ronnie thinks I am way too protective of Michael, and that I need to let him grow up and be a man. It really hurts my feelings that my husband isn't taking me seriously. "Okay," I reluctantly agree.

I try to convince myself that I am just overanxious, and that everything will be all right, but I am haunted by Michael's puzzling words to us just before we left.

As we continue on my route, I replay in my mind the events of this weekend. Michael spent Friday night with his friend, Daniel, and was to come home Saturday to help Ronnie with yard work. But we didn't hear from him until 12:30 A. M. Sunday morning.

The phone rang. I answered, and Michael said, "Hi Mom, can you come pick me up?"

Peeved at his apparent thoughtlessness, I answered, "No, I am not going to stop what I'm doing, but I'll send your daddy."

About 15 minutes later, I heard the front door swing open, and in they came. They were arguing about Michael's staying at Daniel's all day and not calling.

Michael said, "Well, Dad, I tried to call, and there was no answer."

I listened to them for a while, and then reminded them that I had turned the phone off to get some rest.

"Oh, the phone was off?" Ronnie asked. "That's all I needed to know."

A few minutes later my husband was in the bathroom getting dressed. I heard Michael mumble as he passed in the hallway, "You won't have to worry about me much longer."

I didn't think too much about it at the time, but just finished dressing. I guessed that he and Danny might be planning to move into an apartment.

On our way out to run my paper route, I urged Michael, "Come on and go with us this morning, Son."

"Mama, I'm too tired, and I want to go to bed." "Okay," I reluctantly agreed." The last thing I said to him when I walked out the door was, "Michael, I love you."

From his chair in the dark, he replied, "I know, Mom.

I love you, too."

"I love you, to" Ronnie interrupts my thoughts. "Dee, I'm hungry. Please stop at Knight Brothers. I want a biscuit. It won't take but a minute." Irritated, I steer the car into the store parking lot.

"Please hurry up," I snap at Ronnie. "I am worried about Michael." As I wait in the car, Ronnie's "short time" seems endless.

We finally pull into our driveway about 6 AM, and I jump out hurry to the door and burst into an eerily quiet kitchen. I rush down the hallway straight towards Michael's room. I usually check on him and his younger sister, Rhonda, as soon as I get home. But today is different. I never make it to Rhonda's room, because I stop at Michael's bedroom first.

Opening his door the light from the hallway illuminated his dark room. I see Michael's legs and he's still wearing his white socks, white surfer shirt and black shorts. What in the world? He must have had another seizure and slid off his black satin sheets.

I yell for my husband. "Ronnie, come help me! Michael's half on the floor. Can you help me pull him back on his mattress?"

I step over his legs and turn on his desk lamp.

As I turn back towards the door, my son's twisted torso is lying on his right side, and his head is under his pillow. I see the gunstock between his knees. The shock of seeing that shot gun scares me out of my wits. Ronnie casually walks into the room.

"Ronnie, what is Michael doing with that gun?" As I reach to move his pillow to help him back on his bed, Ronnie grabs my arm. He immediately sees the whole story. "Diane, whatever you do, don't touch him!" I turn to look at my husband and watch the blood drain from his face. Suddenly I *know*. My son is dead!

Ronnie wraps his arms around me to keep me from falling and pulls me into the hallway. He didn't want me to see how badly Michael was messed up. We both begin to scream and wail. Our loud noises awaken Rhonda who yells for us to be quiet so she can sleep. She has no clue. Ronnie and I try to calm down, but we continue to sob and hold each other.

"Ronnie, please go help Rhonda, and I will call 911." While I am dialing 911 Rhonda runs out of her room and into Michael's room. She shrieks wildly and I hear her daddy trying to restrain her from touching Michael. Finally she collapses in the hallway and pulls Ronnie down with her. They both lie in the floor and cry their hearts out.

I am so hysterical that the 911 dispatcher can barely understand what I am saying.

She continues to ask me questions---name, address, the problem.

Doesn't she understand I have to get back to my husband and daughter? I'm done with the questions. I finally scream into the phone, "My son is dead! He has committed suicide!"

Ronnie

I recalled that when Kelly was three, Diane and I decided to have another child. I would have been happy with a healthy girl or boy, but I really wanted a boy. I was so excited about Diane's pregnancy, and wanted to be a part of all of it, including the birth.

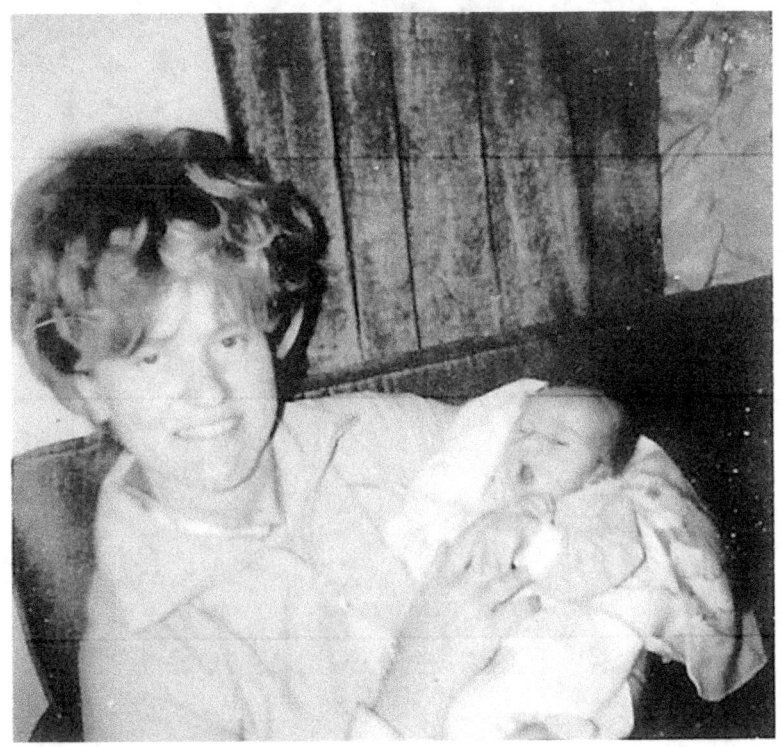

Mike was a long lanky boy, and I just knew he was going to grow up and make me proud of him and have kids and carry on the family name. That's what most fathers want. Sometimes things have a way of working out opposite of the way you plan.

CHAPTER 2

After I call 911, my mind shuts down for a little while because I can't face the reality of Michael's death. This is the worst day of my life. I have to find something to do. As I wash the newspaper ink off my hands, it dawns on me that strangers are on their way to my house. I frantically begin to straighten the kitchen and den and change my ink-stained clothes.

A stream of officials begins to arrive---the rescue squad, county sheriffs, and the EMT team. After a deputy questions me about what happened, he suggests that Rhonda and I move to another area of the house to make way for the investigation.

As we sit on the front porch, a highway patrolman pulls up, walks past us, quietly nods, and goes into the house.

Moments later he goes back to his car and returns with a roll of yellow crime scene tape. Seeing the tape really scares me. My mind is racing. "Do they use that yellow tape when it's a suicide?

Why is Ronnie still in Michael's room with all of the police? What are they doing in there? Do they think this is a crime scene?

Do they think we had something to do with it?" All I know is that I can't face what is in that room and I don't want Rhonda to go back in there either.

As Rhonda and I continue to sit on the porch, I notice it is a beautiful Sunday morning. The sun is shining, and the clouds are white and fluffy.

People begin to ride by, slow down and gawk at us as if we are on exhibit. "Rhonda, please, let's go inside and wait in the den." The possibility of us watching the paramedics remove Michael's body fills me with horror.

A stranger walks in and sits down in our straight back chair in the corner. He introduces himself as the chaplain for the sheriff's department. "Your son loved you very much," he says.

His comment infuriates me. Enraged, I start crying. "How can you say such a thing when my son is lying in his room dead?" The chaplain calmly answers, "Because he covered his face with a pillow. He didn't want you to walk in and see him, and remember him that way. I can tell that your son wanted to protect you. I have been to many suicide scenes. When victims are angry with others, they want their loved ones to see what they have done to themselves."

The chaplain continues to counsel us for a few minutes, but he's not getting through and finally left us alone. The last time I saw my son alive, he was sitting in that very same chair telling me how much he loved me. Was it all a lie? If he loved me, would he have done this to us? Done it to himself?

I can't stay in this house a minute longer, I ask, "Rhonda, will you go with me to your sister's and to Granny's?

"Yeah, Mama, but I've got to get some cigarettes first.

Michael came into my room sometime in the middle of the night and woke me up to ask me if he could have a cigarette. You know, Mama, he even told me he loved me."

"Yeah, Baby Girl, that was the last thing he said to me, too."

"Mama, I couldn't find my cigarettes, so I went back into Michael's room looking for them before the police got here. While I was in there I picked up his pillow and looked at him. I was expecting his head to be blown apart, but he looked so calm, Mama. I didn't see much blood."

"I didn't see his face, Rhonda, I just saw the blood puddle in his ear.

Diane

One Christmas morning when Michael was still a toddler, he ran down the hall into the living room and slid across our hardwood floor right up to the edge of the Christmas tree. His brown eyes sparkled with excitement as he focused in on the clear cellophane-covered box that held the very thing that he had asked Santa for—a black and white cowboy suit and all the trimmings. He tore the package open, plopped his new black hat on his head, put his silver bullets in his belt, and holstered his guns. Then he pulled on his cowboy boots and finished opening the rest of his presents. Later on that morning, I dressed him in his complete outfit which he wore the rest of the day.

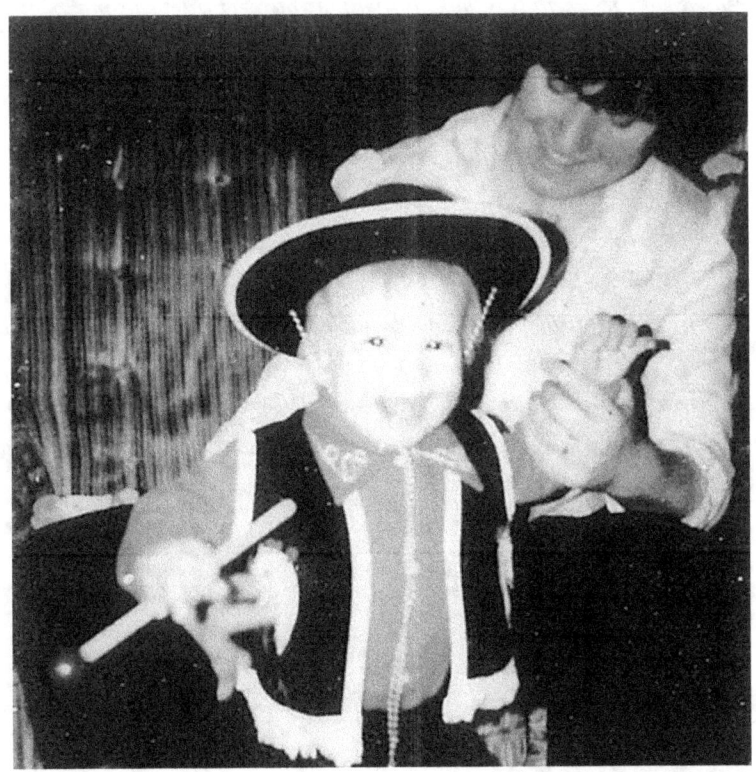

Christmas night I gave him a bath, dressed him in his footy pajamas and put him to bed.

Michael had recently graduated from the crib to a little boy's bed, so I made a point to check on him often. As I peeked around the corner into his room, he was lying on his back, asleep on top of the covers. All I could see were his little feet in his cowboy boots, with the toes sticking straight up. I gently slipped his boots off, trying not to wake him, and stood them quietly beside his bed before leaving the room.

A little while later when I checked on him, there hewas, sleeping like an angel, with those boots on again! I gave up.

The next morning I sat Michael down on the kitchen chair and had a talk with him about his boots. I pulled off his boots, his pajama bottoms and began to rub his little feet. "Just look at how red and creased your feet and legs look, Baby. Do your feet hurt this morning?"

Michael shook his head. No way was he going to admit they hurt. "You see how red and wrinkled your feet are, Sweetheart. Mommy just cannot let you sleep in your boots. Sleeping in your boots may hurt your feet. Do you understand?"

"Okay, Mommy, I not sleep in my boots no more," he answered sweetly.

He just melted my heart. I was so proud that he understood.

Boy was I wrong! That night and every night thereafter, he wore his boots to bed. Over and over I would go in and take them off.

He would wake up and put his boots back on. I tried to reason with him each morning during our little foot-rubbing ritual, and finally gave up.

I cut the feet off all his pajamas, put socks on him and let him sleep in those boots until he out grow them.

CHAPTER 3

Rhonda and I stop back by Knight Brothers' convenience store. I wait to pay at the register and notice cars pulling in and out, people pumping gas, buying newspapers and drinks. Everything looks normal, but our lives have stopped. Rhonda and I are frozen in time. We will never be the same. Never.

First we go to my daughter Kelly's house. Finding the back door unlocked, we walk in and climb the stairs. I call her name from the hallway. "Kelly!" She comes out of her bedroom wearing her nightgown and stops when she sees our faces. Rhonda and I break down and begin crying.

"Mama, what's wrong? Is it Daddy?" "No, Kelly. It's Michael."

Kelly looks frustrated, even disgusted and angrily fires off questions. "What has he done now? Is he in trouble again? Has he been in a car accident? Is he hurt?" "Oh, Kelly, Michael is dead! He killed himself!" Kelly is shocked and rushes to me. We fall into each other's arms, sob, and hold each other up. The girls have to help me down the stairs to the kitchen, and we sit down at the table. After we calm down a little and are able to stop crying, Kelly asks, "What happened, Mama?"

"We don't know, Kelly." I am agitated, wringing my hands, and struggling to breathe. I have been up all night and am completely exhausted.

"Your daddy and I came home from work and found him in his room. He shot himself, Kelly."

"How in the world did he get a gun? I know you and Daddy always padlock your bedroom before you leave."

"Yes, we always lock our room because of those two guns and our medicines. I hate those guns and hate Ronnie's having them.

While we were dressing in the bathroom, Michael slipped into our bedroom, and unlocked the patio door so he could get his shotgun after we left for work."

"How do you know he did that, Mama?"

"Well, we found the outside door unlocked, and the bedroom door was still padlocked, so that's the only way he could have gotten in our room without breaking a window," I explain.

Although I have calmed down a little, Kelly and Rhonda still have to help me walk across the back yard to Mama's to tell her that her youngest grandson is dead.

Mama keeps her doors locked, so we knocked. She opens the storm door, dressed to the nines and ready to go to church.

What's the matter, Diane? What's happened?"

I break down crying and blurt out, "Mama, Michael has committed suicide!"

Not comprehending, she cries out, "What are you saying, Diane?"

"Michael is dead, Mama. He shot himself."

Her face crumbles. Again we all start wailing, hugging and comforting each other as best we can. I am so weak from crying that I collapse in a chair at the dining room table.

Mama changes clothes, puts on a pot of coffee and starts digging in the refrigerator to throw a meal together. We always turn to food for comfort.

"Mama, what am I going to do?" We have no money and no burial insurance. How many families are prepared to bury their 20-year old sons anyway? "Mama, can I use the family plot to bury Michael?"

"I don't think there will be a problem, Diane. I will call the cemetery office tomorrow and find out what I have to do."

"Thank you, Mama." I breathed a sigh of relief. "Can I stay here with you? I can't go back to that house. I don't think I can ever, ever go back. It isn't my home anymore."

"I understand, Diane. You all can stay as long as you need to." I desperately hope she can fix this and tell me what to do, but this time I don't think even my Mama can make it better.

Diane

When Michael was in third grade, we moved from the city to rural Gray's Creek. Michael had loved urban life—lots of kids to play with. Moving to a small community upset his social life. He loved being with people, just like me, and we were both lonely.

Rhonda and Kelly made friends with the girls next door, but there were no young boys in our new neighborhood to play with Michael. In the city he came home from school and had a yard full of friends. In Gray's Creek he came home to stare at the walls or watch TV. Michael had no close friends nearby, his grades dropped and he goofed off at school. Michael was depressed.

Ronnie suggested he sign up for Little League baseball that spring to get him away from the TV. Michael really wasn't a sports jock, but he enjoyed playing and making friends. North Carolina baseball weather is sweltering, but I couldn't bear to miss his first game, even if I had to go alone. Ronnie couldn't be in the sun because of the medicine he was taking. Although I was uncomfortable being by myself, I went anyway. I didn't know anybody at the ball field, nobody knew me, and so I sat alone on the top bleacher.

Michael came up for bat. He wasn't a very good hitter, but that night he got lucky. The pitcher put the ball over the plate; Michael swung with all his might and hit a home run. Everyone went wild cheering.

Instead of running from base to base, Michael was hopping up and down like a jackrabbit. He ran to the next base, looks to see where the ball was and took off again. It was hilarious. We were all laughing and hollering, "Go Michael, go!"

I will never forget the look on his face as he crossed home plate. He was one happy kid. A man on the bleachers in front of me hollered out, "I don't know who that little boy belongs to, but he is one excited little boy!"

I tapped the man on the shoulder and proudly said, "That little boy is Michael Mobley. That boy belongs to me."

CHAPTER 4

I'm worried. Ronnie still hasn't called. I dial the house and ask him what's going on.

"Honey, I can't talk right now," Ronnie says hurriedly. "The paramedics are taking Michael out. I'll call you soon."

Ten minutes later he calls back. "Ronnie, are you coming to Mama's? I can't go back out there."

"Not right now, Diane. I need to stay here and straighten up the rest of the house because people will be coming in."

"Are you going to clean Michael's room?" "No, I don't think I can do that," he answered.

"Well, what are we going to do? I can't do it either." "I understand, honey. We'll discuss it when I get to your Mama's."

I call my friend, Donna. She comes to help me, takes over, and organizes all the phone calls and food. I then call our church to let them know that Michael is dead and how he died.

Suddenly remembering that Michael had volunteered to be an organ donor, I call the hospital who notifies the procurement company to make the proper arrangements.

In less than an hour, I hear a knock on the front door. It's Carrie Dean, a faithful friend from church. She walks in and without saying a word she kneels beside my chair. She holds me as we both sob from the deepest part of our hearts until I feel numb. The tears flow freely until both of our blouses are damp. We finally stop crying. I take a deep breath and relax a little. Carrie Dean moves back, still touching my arm. She doesn't say anything. She just listens as I blurt out, "Carrie Dean, what have I done to deserve such things happening to me and my family?" She has a blank look on her face. After a few seconds, she says, "Diane, the enemy comes to steal, kill, and destroy, and that is all I know. I don't understand how. Sometimes I just don't understand." After pondering what she said for a few moments, I answer by shaking my head from side to side, "Neither do I, Carrie Dean, neither do I."

Carrie Dean stands up beside my chair, moves over and sits down on the couch. We had cried all we could. Regaining my composure I ask, "Carrie Dean, how did you get here so fast?"

"The church secretary called to tell me that Michael had killed himself. Earl and I were getting ready to leave the house. I told him that I had to go to you, so I dropped him off at the church, and told Pastor that I was going to the Mobley's."

I was puzzled. "How in the world did you find me since I wasn't home?"

"When I left the church, all I could think of was getting to you, Diane. I drove several miles out Highway 87 before I realized that I didn't know where you lived. I then called the church to find out how to get to your house and was told that you were at your Mother's."

"Thank you for coming, Carrie Dean. When I look back, you have always shown up when I have had a major crisis in my life. You just don't know what it means to me for you to be here."

Carrie Dean is the first in a long line of people who come and go, but I have no recollection of most of the visitors.

When Ronnie arrives at Mama's, we go to her bedroom for privacy because this is the first time we have been alone. We fall into each other's arms and cry like babies.

"Oh, Ronnie, why did he do this? Didn't he know that we loved him, that we would have done anything to help him, that no problem was so big that we couldn't have worked it out?"

"Michael knew that we loved him, Diane. The sheriff found a yellow Post-It note lying on the night stand under Michael's arm. I left the note in the china cabinet at the house because I was afraid that something would happen to it."

"What did it say, Ronnie?"

"It said, 'I'm sorry for all the pain I have caused, but I just can't take it anymore. At least this is the last pain I will ever cause you. I love you very much. Mike Mobley.'"

I feel my heart break in two. How can I live with this? Michael is gone! I can't help him now. He left me with no options. I would have moved heaven and earth to ease his pain, to get him help, to do whatever it took. He must have been so tortured. How could I not have known? How could he think that his death could possibly make things better for us?

"Did we cause this?" I ask Ronnie as he holds me in his arms. "Was it something that we did to make him think that suicide was the only way out for him?"

"No, Dee, we are good parents, but Mike had a lot of problems."

We sit silently on the side of Mama's bed for a long time. My mind wanders to other things. "Ronnie, why were you in Michael's room so long?"

"Honey, when anyone has been shot, there is suspicion of foul play, so the police asked me a lot of questions."

"What kind of questions?"

"Like why Michael would have killed himself, if he had any problems, if we'd had an argument, things like that."

"Sure he had problems! But that was no reason for him to kill himself, is it?" Ronnie shakes his head and continues to hold me.

"Did you ever look at Michael's face, Ronnie?"

Reluctantly he responds. He doesn't want to tell me what he saw and chooses his words carefully. "Yes, I looked at him before the police came when Rhonda and I were in his room. I felt his arms and his face, and I checked to see if he was breathing."

"What did he look like? Was there a lot of blood?" I ask numbly.

"No, Diane, there was no exit wound, but there was a little swelling around his mouth. The blood I saw was right under his chin and a puddle in his ear."

Instantly I am back in the bedroom. I can see that pillow again, covering Michael's face and his blood. Dark blood. I want to run and hide. Escape the pain. It is so raw and hurts so bad. I want to crawl in a hole and die, but we have decisions to make.

"What are we going to do about his room, Ronnie?" Ronnie suggests that we ask our son-in-law, Jeff, and his father, Jerry, to clean up Michael's room. They agree to help us and leave with Ronnie to go back to the house.

Later that afternoon I am sitting on the front porch in the swing with Pam, my best friend from high school. My pastor arrives and sits down in the rocking chair in front of us. Thankful to see him, I ask if he will conduct the funeral. We discuss arrangements, and I also ask him if his son will sing "How Great Thou Art," and "Amazing Grace." He agrees, and we finish making our plans.

As I watch Pastor pull out of the driveway, I realize he can't help me any more than my Mama can. Besides losing Michael today, I have lost the joy of living. The song in my heart is gone, as if a murderous claw has torn into my chest, ripped my heart out, and left nothing but a gaping hole.

Diane

One day when Michael was in Ms. Butler's sixth grade class at Gray's Creek Elementary School, he came home all excited. "Son," I asked, "What have you got in that big bag?" "It's my Santa Claus suit for the play, Mama!"

"You got the Santa part in the play? Is that the main role?" "Yeah, Mama, I had already memorized all the words before I tried out for the part, so the teacher said I could do it." "Congratulations, son, I am really proud of you."

Holding up a giant pair of red pants, he asked, "How in the world am I going to keep these big things on? You gotta help me, Mama. What are we gonna do?

"Well, Honey, we can't have a skinny Santa Claus, so we'll have to stuff those pants with a pillow."

On the night of the play as I helped him dress, we realized there was no belt with the Santa suit, so we had to rush around looking for one. We couldn't find a big black belt anywhere, so finally settled for one of his Dad's belts that came with a hook clasp instead of a buckle.

"Mama, do you think this belt is going to stay hooked? I don't want my pants to fall off in front of everyone. I'd be the laughingstock of the whole school!"

"I don't know, Michael," I said while hurriedly stuffing the pillow under his shirt and down his pants, "but this is what we're going to do. Pull your shirt up and let me put this other belt around your pillow to hold it up, and all we can do is pray that none of it comes loose."

At Seven PM, every seat in the school auditorium was filled with parents and kids. The air was charged with a joy and excitement that you could almost taste. The Christmas play was about to begin.

As the curtains rose, we saw all the children on stage dressed in their festive holiday clothes, sitting around, chatting and waiting for Santa.

Out came Michael swinging his big belly from side to side, and shouting, "Ho, Ho, Ho, Merry Chr "

Before he could finish his sentence, his belt popped off and went flying. Michael froze. The startled look on his face which translated (Oops! I may lose my pants any second), caused the audience to just crack up laughing.

In a split-second, he remembered the other belt that I had put under his shirt to hold everything together. Without missing a beat and with a big smile, Mr. Cool nonchalantly re-established his authority on that stage.

He gathered up his belt, hooked it around his waist, turned to the audience, and in a loud voice proclaimed, "Ho, Ho, Ho, Merry Christmas!"

I later asked his teacher why she chose Michael for the part of Santa and she said because Michael was the only student that was able to remember all the words.

CHAPTER 5

The next morning Michael was supposed to report to the Sheriff's Office at 6 A.M. I call their number at six on the dot. A lady answered, "May I help you?"

"This is Diane Mobley, Michael Mobley's mother. I'm sorry. Michael won't be there today."

She cut me off and snapped, "He will report or I will dispatch a sheriff to pick him up right away."

"Then you'll have to go to the morgue and pick him up" I shrieked, "because he's dead!"

Dead silence followed. She apologized and didn't really know what else to say. I hung up.

After Michael's autopsy is performed and his donor tissues harvested, his body is sent to the mortuary on Monday afternoon.

Michael is to be buried in the black suit that he had worn to his sister Kelly's wedding. In all the funeral decisions we make, we pick out things Michael would have loved. We choose a bronze casket and fall-colored casket spray because Michael loved autumn colors. When he was alive, we drove around, looked at all the beautiful fall foliage, and loved the nip in the air.

A number of Michael's friends agree to be pallbearers. I know my son's death is not their fault, but some of them are involved with drugs, and I resent that they are alive and that my son is dead. Why my son?

On the other hand, I want them to realize what happened to Michael can easily happen to them unless they quit using drugs and get their lives straightened out. I just want them to feel some of the pain I feel. Extreme pain is causing me to be unfair, but I'm mad and blaming everyone.

My nerves are shattered, so our family physician calls in a prescription for me. Every time I feel like I am going to lose it or start screaming, I take another pill.

Late Tuesday morning the funeral home staff calls to tell us that Michael is ready for the family to view.

Ronnie says, "Diane, come on, let's go."

"No, Ronnie, I don't want to see him. I just can't go. I don't want a vision of Michael lying dead in a casket to be my last memory of our son."

"Diane, please come with us," Ronnie begs. "Just leave me alone. I am not going."

So Ronnie and Rhonda go to view the body without me.

When they return, Ronnie says, "Diane, he doesn't look that bad. You need to go see him." For over half an hour he pleads with me to go to the funeral home, and I finally give in just to get him to shut up.

When I get out of the car and start toward the funeral home, I feel like I am walking to my death. It is horrible.

I am scared to look at Michael, afraid of what I will see. It is a relief when I see the body, because it doesn't look like my son. Michael has a narrow face, but this jaw line is way too wide. Who is this stranger? I hadn't thought to take a picture of Michael to the funeral director.

The director suggests that we have a closed casket during the wake. She explains that though there were no visible wounds, the bird shot from the 410/gauge shotgun did a great deal of damage inside his head--- lots of shattered bones and teeth.

His skull had to be packed to give some shape to his lower face. She further explains that the autopsy and removal of donor tissue have caused the embalming fluid to leak. They were forced to put Michael in a plastic bag.

Has this woman lost her mind? I want to go across the desk and choke her.

Does she not realize that this is MY SON she is talking about? Michael's body lies leaking in plastic, like meat thawing in the refrigerator.

Grandmother Irene

When Michael was about three, we went to a play Kelly was in at Brentwood Elementary. Some ladies behind us were carrying on a conversation, and said to him, "You sure are a pretty boy." Michael smiled up at them with an angelic smile and said, "Yeah, I know."

Michael was the only grandchild I had who would come give me a hug when he walked in the door.

He often told me he that he loved me and when he grew up he was going to buy me a Grand Am.

CHAPTER 6

Tuesday morning my sister Kaye flies home from California. Later that afternoon Ronnie and I return from the funeral home. We all sit at the dining room table eating and talking. "Ronnie, we have to go tomorrow and pay for Michael's flowers." My sister interrupts our conversation, "No, you don't, Diane, I have already paid for the casket spray and for digging Michael's grave." "Kaye, you didn't have to do that."

"I know, but I wanted to help." After you and Ronnie left, Mama and I decided to go to the florist, and we paid for the flowers. Then we went to sign the papers at the cemetery, so you can use one of her plots to bury Michael. While we were there, I asked how much it would cost to dig the grave and decided to take care of it for you.

"How much did they charge, Kaye?"

"It was six hundred dollars and I knew it was something I could do."

"Thank you, Sis. I will pay you back as soon as I can." "No, I don't want you to do that."

When she sees the doubt on my face, she pleads, "Please let me do this for you, Sweetie."

"OK, Sis, I really appreciate it." Although I don't say it to her, it means so much to me to have such a wonderful sister who deeply loves my whole family.

The night of the wake I take a picture of Michael to the funeral home and place it on the marble stand beside the closed casket. It was his eleventh grade picture. He is so handsome, but for the first time I notice how sad his eyes looked. The somber expression on his face fits the mood of the evening, as if he is grieving with us.

All of the sudden I realize Ronnie has left me to greet other people and I panic. I stand alone in the middle of the room lost in a sea of faces, many of them I don't know. Ronnie is my anchor. Turning my back to the casket, I take a deep breath and play the role of hostess. I begin to greet, laugh, talk and enjoy friends that I haven't seen in a long time. It's my way of pretending that the casket doesn't exist and that Michael is not dead. I pop another little white pill. I have no idea what my doctor prescribed, but thank goodness for prescription drugs. Without these pills I would turn into a screaming maniac.

Ronnie joins me again as Rhonda and Kelly walk up. "Daddy, "Rhonda says, "Some of Michael's friends want to see him one last time. Can we please open the casket?"

"Baby Girl, they strongly recommended we not open it." "I know, Daddy, but we just want to tell him goodbye."

"Okay, I'll go see what I can do, but don't get your hopes up."

After a few minutes of discussion with the funeral director, Ronnie comes back over. "They agree to open the casket only if we agree to allow two gentlemen to stand guard at opposite ends of the casket."

"What? Why? I've never heard of such a thing." "Calm down, Diane, "Ronnie says, "It's for Michael's protection, and they don't want people jostling the plastic bag because of the odor."

Lots of teenagers and their parents decide to stay. Mama, my friend Myrtle, and I sit on the couch across the room from the casket. As two men approach the casket all conversation stops. Dead silence. They raise the lid.

Rhonda and Myrtle's daughter, Ronette, who are childhood friends, hesitantly walk over together to look at Michael. Wailing they hold each other up. Myrtle and I jump up to comfort them, and lead them away from the casket.

I never look at Michael again. Thank God Ronnie pressured me into looking at Michael's body yesterday. I could not bear knowing that my last memory of my son would have been his lying on his bed, dead, with that shotgun between his legs.

Kaye

"I remember how excited he was at Christmas time. One year he wanted a skate board, and rather than send him the money through the mail, I decided to pick it out myself. I took my own children, John and Jamie, to help me pick out the decals and whatnot. John, who was just a few years older than Michael, loved skate boarding, and he picked out the most popular type board of the day.

When Michael got it, he called me long distance. You could hear the excitement in his voice over the telephone. It was always such a pleasure to give Michael things because he was always so appreciative."

CHAPTER 7

The morning of the funeral I realize that I only own one dress and it is too small. I have to go shopping.

All my accessories are in the house at Gray's Creek, so I have no choice but to go back. I'm running late and when I get home, Ronnie's family is already there waiting for me. I hurriedly dress, and we all go to Mama's and climb into the two limousines to ride in total silence the whole way to the funeral home.

I haven't slept in four days and am totally exhausted. Walking into the funeral home chapel, I see the casket, our pastor, and the pastor from Green Springs. I feel the sympathetic expressions of our extended family and friends, and the judgmental stares of others.

As my pastor begins to preach the service, I recall our earlier conversation in which he had asked me if I had any preferences as to what he preached.

I said, "Yes, will you please speak to the living? Michael is dead and gone. You can't help him, Pastor, but I want Michael's young friends to hear about the love of God. "

So that's what he does. He talks to the living. His son sings the two songs we requested. The rest of the funeral is a blur. The service ends. Our family files out of the chapel, and I notice the sympathetic looks on the faces of some of my friends and feel their love.

It's a beautiful, warm, sunny November day, like a little gift from God. No coats or jackets. The last warm weather before the cold sets in. Today is the kind of day I would have enjoyed if I wasn't sitting in this graveyard burying my son. My family has spent many Sunday afternoons in this same place having a wonderful time feeding the ducks. In fact it wasn't long ago that Michael, Rhonda and I brought my grandson, Jon, out here.

Who would have thought a month later I'd be here sitting in front of Michael's casket?

Now everything is surreal and confusing. Can this really be my son? What am I doing here? How did I let things go this far? I have no answers.

Although the preacher finishes his last prayer, nobody moves. Nobody knows what to say. I sit there for a moment, but it seems like an eternity. My standing up is a pivotal point for me that day. As soon as I stand, I refuse to accept that my son is dead. There is nothing here for me. I turn and make my way to the limousine.

I have no idea how I get there, but I find myself watching from inside the car as people begin to approach Ronnie to talk with him. My pain and devastation are so personal that I just cannot let people see. If even one person approaches me with pity or compassion, I know I will go over the edge, and I don't know if I can get back. If I let go of my emotions and show what I am feeling, I will go stark raving crazy and shatter into little pieces.

Yvonne

The night I met Diane Mobley we were at an all-night prayer vigil at church. It was about 1 AM and we took a break, sat on the floor, talking and introducing ourselves to each other.

When Diane told me her name, I was so excited and exclaimed, "You are Michael Mobley's mother? I have wanted to meet you. I've got a fantastic story about your son!"

Diane just smiled and asked, "Well, what have you got to say about my sweet boy?"

"Well, Diane, this homeless lady came to our children's church meeting and appealed to the kids to help her buy some gifts for her children who were staying in a local orphanage. I had allowed her

to come because she needed help, but also to teach our young people about giving.

She talked to us about her children and so we took up an offering. I thought we would just get their little pennies and nickels which would have been just fine.

But I was surprised to see Michael had given a ten dollar bill. I was pleased but very concerned that he had put in more money than his parents would be pleased with, so I quietly pulled him aside and asked, "Michael, this is such a wonderful thing you did! Where did you get so much money?"

"I got it for my birthday, Miss Yvonne."

"Do you think your parents might be unhappy that you gave all this money away?"

He smiled so sweetly, "No, Miss Yvonne. If my Mama was here she'd do the same thing. My Mama taught me to help people."

As I told Diane this story I could see her swelling with pride. "Well, I am so glad to know I am getting through to him. It is true that we don't have a lot of money. It was really for something for him to wear, but he gave out of his need. He has a Mom and Dad and a house to live in and saw a family who was worse off than we were and needed help."

As she spoke to me, I was also reminded of something else about Michael. "Diane, do you realize how wonderful your son is? Not only is he tender hearted, he is smart as a whip. Just the other night in class I finally had to ask him to slow down a little and let some of the other children answer some of the Bible questions. He seems to know every Bible story we cover, and all kinds of verses.

"Oh yes, we read together every night. Once he heard something, he never forgot it. I always wondered where this smart kid came from." Both of us laughed, and then we turned back to the altar and began to pray.

CHAPTER 8

C urled up in the back seat of the limo, I feel like an animal in pain that has crawled into its cave.

The tinted windows create an illusion of darkness, the perfect place for me to hide. Peering through the window all I can see are my friends and family chatting and visiting with each other. Suddenly the concerned driver snatches the door open and asks, "Are you okay?"

"Fine," I lied, but I really wanted to bite his head off. What a stupid question! How could any mother be okay who just buried her son?

As Ronnie, Kelly, Rhonda, Mama and Kaye silently get back into the car; I study the pain in each face. I've been so wrapped up in my own feelings. I finally realize that they need me to help them though this horror. How will I ever be able to make this any better?

Ronnie puts his arm around my shoulders and holds my hand as we pull out of the cemetery. "Diane, are you coming home today or staying at your Mom's?"

"There's no way I am going to that house now, and I don't know if I will ever be able to go back." I say emphatically.

As night falls everyone leaves Mama's, and the silence is deafening. Up to this moment, I've been insulated by the love of family and friends. Now I have a decision to make. Do I go home to my husband and daughter, or do I walk away and never look back? I realize there is no choice. Because I love my family, I have to go home, back to that hell hole.

It is a long drive home. Every minute of the ride I dread walking back into the house. I pull into the driveway. I am scared to get out of the car, knowing I have to face the reality of Michael's room. I am afraid of what I will see. What horror is lurking behind his bedroom door?

Standing outside his door, I pray for the courage to open it. I slowly turn the knob and ease my way in. The room is empty except for Michael's desk and night stand. The bed and bedding are gone. The blood has been wiped up, but the stain is indelibly soaked into the grain and cracks of our hardwood floor.

Panicking, I rush to the kitchen and fix a pan of hot, soapy water and get an old rag. Back to his room I go to erase all the evidence of Michael's suicide. I am on my hands and knees, crying hysterically, scrubbing as hard as I can.

Ronnie comes in. "Diane, what are you doing? Get up. Don't do that tonight. Leave it for later."

"I've got to do it. If I am going to sleep in this house tonight, this blood has got to go! Ronnie, I cannot live in this house!" I continue to scrub the stain that will not come up.

"We can't leave, honey. We can't afford it. We don't have any money."

"Don't you understand that I will die if I stay in this house?"

"No, you're not going to die, Dee," Ronnie tries to assure me.

"We will help each other through this. We will survive."

I tune him out and continue to scrub. My husband doesn't have a clue. He has no idea that with each pointless stroke of the rag, I plot ways to take my own life. Swallow too many pills? Slam my car into a tree? How could I do it so it would look like an accident? What method could I use that wouldn't hurt my family?

Pondering ways to take my own life, I stop and think, "What is wrong with you, Diane? You can't kill yourself. Your family will not survive another suicide. Michael, you didn't have the courage to live, but I do. I have to be strong." Maybe if I tell myself this every day, I will start to believe it.

Abi

Michael and I became good friends in 1994 during youth meetings at Green Springs Baptist Church. Michael was nineteen and so tall! He used to grab me around the neck and rub on my head with his fist. And I would think "oh, no"! It would mess up my hair and that's the last thing a fourteen year old girl wants done-- her hair messed up.

Michael always treated me like a little sister. I think he liked the idea that I was sweet, innocent, church girl, and he encouraged me to stay that way.

Michael was a good person, very loving and caring. We spent a lot of time in church together for over six months. He was also outspoken. If he had an opinion, you knew it. He enjoyed people, but he didn't care to have the spotlight on himself. He would rather help you, and see you shine.

Helping others made him feel good. I loved Michael's voice when he sang. I remember he used to always sing this pop song "More than Words." When he and his best friend got together, they were so funny. They had us rolling with laughter. We younger ones couldn't help but love them because we thought they were so cool.

CHAPTER 9

I've barely slept since I found Michael's body. On Monday afternoon I am still in my nightgown, sitting at the dining room table. It's all I can do to avoid re-living the horrific nightmare I had last Saturday. I had dreamed that I was violently and repeatedly raped by an intruder. It seemed so real that I am still petrified to walk into my bedroom, much less try to sleep in there.

My thoughts are interrupted as Ronnie walks in and says, "Honey, get dressed. We're going downtown to the Sheriff's Department."

"Whatever for?"

"Well, when the police left last Sunday, they said I could go pick up my shotgun after it was processed. It's been a week, so I am going to go get it."

"Ronnie, you know I hate that gun. What are you going to do with it?"

"Well, I'm going to put it back in the bedroom where it's always been."

"Are you crazy?"

Calmly Ronnie answers, "No, Diane. We've already lost Michael and can't change that, but I am not giving up that gun, too."

"Yes you are, Ronnie! I don't want it in the house. If the shotgun hadn't been here in the first place, Michael couldn't have used it!"

"Diane, I just don't feel the way you do about it. Back when I was growing up on the farm, our family always had hunting rifles. This particular gun has been in my family for years and it's valuable. I will continue to keep it locked in our room for safety reasons. I hate that you feel bad about it, but I want my gun back."

I finally give up. Ronnie is very calm- a bottom-line man, and I am very emotional about this issue. I will try to deal with this when I'm stronger.

Still, I can't get it off my mind as we ride into town towards the Sheriff's office. I've calmed down and realized I have no options. Just have to learn to live with it.

Ronnie interrupts my thoughts. "Honey, I've been thinking about everything you said. It's not the gun's fault. The gun is just an object, but it was my fault for not checking the bedroom doors before I left."

I can't bear for my husband to take the blame so I said, "No Ronnie. It wasn't your fault. Remember you told me you walked into our room on several occasions and found our outside bedroom door unlocked? I also found some shotgun shells in Michael's room a couple of times when I was cleaning. Each time I picked them up and put them back in the shell box. Ronnie, do you think, he was planning his death the whole time?

"I just don't know, honey. I just don't know."

We pull into the parking lot, find a handicap space, get out of our Nissan truck and head towards the court house to pick up the gun. Ronnie thinks this is resolved, but I know that every time I see that shotgun, I will see the stock sticking out from between Michael's legs.

Kim

Michael and I met in youth group at Fayetteville Community Church. He ended up being one of my very best friends. We had a special friendship. He was the one person in my life I wanted to share everything with as soon as it happened, good and bad. We talked every single day on the phone, and most days more than once.

I have so many memories of Michael. The one thing that stands out in my mind is how protective he was over me, especially when he did not approve of a boy I was interested in. He was like another one of my brothers.

CHAPTER 10

When we walk in from the courthouse, Ronnie heads towards the bedroom with the shotgun.

"I am livid, but I just shut up. If I get started I may not be able to stop. Any hurtful words I say at this point could destroy my marriage. I love my husband, and I don't want to hurt him. God knows he's been hurt enough. But I am still angry, and I want to slap him or somebody! Anybody.

Ronnie props the gun in the corner of our bedroom and comes back out into the den---the very room we last saw Michael alive. "Diane, I think you and I need to sit down and have a talk." Silently, I sit down in my recliner, fold my arms across my chest and wait for him to start. "Honey, you say you would do better if we get away from here," Ronnie says tenderly, "but I am trying to cope with Mike's death, too. I think I will feel closer to Michael by staying in our home. I know you want to move, but since we can't, would it help you if we tear the walls out and do away with Mike's room?"

"Do whatever you want to do, Ronnie. I'm not helping," I say emphatically. "I've worked on this house for 11 years and I'm not doing another thing to it."

Later that week, I hear Ronnie and Rhonda making a racket in Michael's bedroom and get up to see what's going on. They are moving furniture out of his room. Hammers, sledge hammers and crowbars are scattered all over the floor. Ronnie hands me a sledge hammer. "You want to beat on these walls some?"

"It will give me great pleasure to tear these walls down," I said. "I believe I can demolish this whole place right by myself." I sling the hammer with all my might, knock out two walls, throw the sledgehammer down and walk out of that mess. I never help with another bit of it. Rhonda and Ronnie paint and finish the room. Ronnie thinks I will be happy now.

The only thing I did was refurnish the room several times.

I made it a sitting room, then a dining room, and later a playroom for the grandkids. Every time I redecorated the room, I gave the furniture away and started all over. It was a "no man's land" in the middle of my house.

Heath

The first time I heard Michael sing I was deeply moved. He had a very strong, bold voice. And he led us in many of the songs we sang at Green Springs Baptist Church. He also co-wrote a song called "Inside Out." I continue singing this song to this day.

I first found out about Mike's drug problem during a church retreat at Holden's beach. That night we were all awakened by Mike's loud yelling in his sleep. It was frightening to hear him and watch his tossing and turning in his bed. Our leader went in to wake him up and calm him down.

The next morning, while Mike was still asleep, our leader gathered us around to tell us about Mike's drug history. He explained that Mike's past use of drugs still caused him to have seizures periodically. I was shocked. I had no idea Mike had ever done drugs. Our whole group decided we would accept Mike for who he was, and we would continue to pray for him and be his friend.

The last time I saw Mike, we were playing softball in Parkton. Once when I went up to bat, Michael told me something I never forgot. He said, "Heath, things are not always as they seem." I still hold these words dear to my heart as a constant reminder that you never know what you have until it's gone.

CHAPTER II

About six months after Michael died; Ronnie and I decide to go to a movie. After watching the movie for a while, I go to the bathroom. Walking down the hall I turn the corner to the bathrooms. There is a young man talking on the phone with his back to me. My first thought is "it's Michael." He has his baseball cap on backwards. He has on a tee shirt and surfing shorts. He has dark brown hair and from the back he looks just like Michael. It startles me and then I realize it can't be Michael.

I go on into the bathroom, cry for a long time and return to my seat. Ronnie says, "Diane, where have you been?" I don't tell him in the theater, but after the movie I explain what happened near the bathroom. "Ronnie I will be so relieved when that style of dress is gone. Everywhere I see a young man dressed like a surfer, it reminds me of Michael."

Every night when Ronnie goes to bed, I watch TV and wait up for Michael. When it is 11:00 p.m. and he is not home, I face the reality again. He is not ever coming home.

I get hysterical, throw things, beat on the chair, rant and rave until I have no strength left. It has become a habit to get in my car at night and ride and ride and ride for hours with nowhere to go.

The only relief I have from the pain is looking after the babies in the nursery at church. They are my little rays of sunshine. They love on me and I love on them. The nursery was my safe place. I would leave them and go back into darkness. People at the church didn't have a clue what was going on with me. I put a smile on my face and built a wall around my emotions.

Living in this house is driving me crazy. If I had the means I don't know if Ronnie would ever see me again. I want to run away forever. My sunshine has left. I am dying inside. My world is dark and dreary.

The minutes became hours
The hours became days
The days became years.

And the pain never stops.

CHAPTER 12

2002

For eight years our family didn't talk about Michael. We survived from day to day, and just buried the pain. I didn't realize that I had never told anyone what happened that day, not even my counselor who I had weekly meeting during all this time. Once I decided to write this book, to my surprise, no one wanted to talk to me about Michael, the good or the bad. Not his friends, nor our family. It was as if my son had never existed.

Finally my husband agreed to this interview:

RONNIE'S STORY

I remember the night I went to pick up Mike from Daniel's house. It was about midnight as I parked in his driveway. The lights from my truck reflected on Michael's face as he walked towards me. His eyes looked really strange. He got in the truck and said, "Hey Padre."

Even though I was really upset with him, I said, "Hey, how are you? Are you doing okay?"

Mike nonchalantly answered, "I'm fine, Dad."

Mike sensed my irritation right away as I continued to drive home. "Michael, I am upset with you because you didn't come home today and cut the grass like you promised. And furthermore, I expect cooperation from you if you expect me to give you money."

"I know, Dad. I did promise, and I'm sorry."

Mike had a way of sweet talking you to avoid a confrontation, so he changed the subject.

"Dad, I want to go out with my friends tomorrow. There's a dance."

"Michael, you're going to have to be very careful who you associate with while you're on probation. You can go out and have fun, but you aren't supposed to be where there is alcohol or drugs. You have to follow through with what you promised the judge."

He didn't like what I said. "What am I supposed to do, just sit home and twiddle my thumbs?"

When we got home, Mike jumped out of the car, slammed the door, and stomped up the steps into the house. As he walked down the hall he muttered to himself that we wouldn't have to worry about him much longer. I didn't really pay it any mind, just thought he was planning to move out. I had no idea that his seemingly innocent words would shatter the rest of our lives.

When Diane and I got ready to leave for work, I asked, "Are you sure you don't want to go on the route with us?"

"No, I'll be all right. I'm just going to stay here and read a little bit, and go to bed."

"Mike, don't worry about anything that I said or what we discussed. There's no problem that can't be overcome. We'll talk later when I get home. Get some rest, because Monday morning you've got to report to your probation officer, and I will take you down there."

If only I had known that would be the last conversation I would ever have with my son.

CHAPTER 13

After we found Michael dead, the police asked me not to go in or disturb anything. The paramedics and ambulance came to pick up his body. The police asked me a few questions. "Mr. Mobley had you and your son had any arguments recently? Can you think of any reason he might have shot himself?"

As he's asking me, I'm thinking, I don't have a clue. I'm completely bewildered, numb and in shock. "Well, we had a few word, just a small dispute over him not coming home like he should have, but nothing that would have caused him to shoot himself."

I've thought about the police's questions many times over the years. It's so frustrating trying to figure it out, because it's all speculation. Was there something, anything at all I could have done that would have made a difference?

After my wife and daughter left the house, I went out on the front porch and told one of the officers, "I just don't believe Michael would do something like this and not leave a note or tell us something."

Another officer who overheard our conversation came out on the porch and said, "Well, he did leave a note."

As he showed me the note, he asked if it was my son's handwriting. I said, "Yes."

An officer stayed out on the porch with me and I cried for a while. The other officers came out and tried to console me while the ambulance backed up to the door. The paramedics went in and put Mike's body on a stretcher, and covered him up. They rolled him out on the porch.

I asked the officer in charge, "Please! Let me see him."

"Mr. Mobley, it would be better if you didn't see him like this. You've been through enough today."

So the paramedics loaded Mike's body into the ambulance. Another officer came out of the house with the shotgun. "Sir, we need to take the weapon with us because it was used to inflict a wound. You can pick it up later at the station if you like. If not, it will be disposed of."

All that I was able to say was, "Ok." I watched as they all got in their vehicles and drove away. I walked back into the den and broke down crying. When I finally got myself together, I straightened part of the house, got in my truck and left.

I then drove to town to get my son-in-law, Jeff, and his father. They had agreed to clean up everything for us. I just couldn't do it. They took off the bedcovers, got the mattresses out of the house, wiped up all the blood and scrubbed the floor. The blood had clotted and was like a gel on the floor and the mattresses. As they were cleaning up, I heard one of them vomiting, but they finally finished up everything and we left.

CHAPTER 14

D iane refused to come home. The reality was that she just couldn't come back. She used her Mom's home in town as a base because it was more convenient for most of our friends to drop in.

I decided to stay at the house because people were coming to visit and bringing food. I don't remember who all came and went. People wanted to know where Diane was.

After all the well-wishers were gone, and I sat at the house by myself, I began reminiscing about my son.

Even when Michael was young and growing up, I knew that he wanted to be liked, to be everybody's friend. He wasn't a leader. He was a follower. My wife understood Michael so well that I'm sure if those two had been together the week he died, she would have known that he was up to something.

Rhonda and Kelly were close to me. We were able to have fun and laugh and talk about most things, except the subject of boys. They didn't want to know what I had to say about boys. So they asked their mother for advice because she was more sympathetic.

Because of my health, all the kids helped me with the yard work. Kelly enjoyed helping her mom with housework while Rhonda and I both liked fishing, working on the cars, that sort of thing.

On the other hand, Mike and I didn't have much in common. Mike would help with the chores, but yard work was not his favorite way to spend the day. He didn't like getting his hands dirty. He spent his time indoors reading and playing video games.

This was the first of many times I sat and pondered about Mike asking myself what I could have done or said to better understand and help my boy.

One day I went down to the corner store and the owner said to me, "There are rumors going around that you shot and killed your own son, Mr. Mobley."

"Yeah, I heard the same rumor. That's so stupid. I would never consider doing anything like that to my own child. Sure, like I went to Mike's room and forced him to lie down and stick a gun between his legs, and under his chin, and pull the trigger. Not hardly. No one could force anybody to do something like that."

The owner said, "I told that person, there ain't no way Mr. Mobley would do that to one of his kids, not as much as he loved his children."

The owner knew me well. I loved my kids and was there for them even when I had to be tough.

Just like the time I took Mike's driver's license. One day he drove the old surf wagon to pick up Rhonda from school.

Turned right across in front of somebody and then smacked them. Then he totaled Diane's white truck. He also started having seizures. Mike thought I was hard on him sometimes, but I was afraid he would kill somebody or himself.

I remembered another time. It was a summer day in '94, just a few months before he died. We were cooking out at Kelly's and Mike finally showed up late. I asked, "What happened to you?"

"I got lost," he said.

Michael couldn't remember how to get to his sister's. He was definitely disoriented. Anyone whose mind has been affected that much by drugs doesn't need to be driving anyway. And it wasn't just the driving causing problems. It was the stealing, too.

CHAPTER 15

M ike couldn't keep a job because of his stealing. Of course, crack and other drugs made Mike do things he ordinarily wouldn't do. We now believe that Mike or some of his friends stole our missing items to buy crack.

We also think he was fired at the leather goods store for stealing. There was an incident when we had to wait over an hour in the mall parking lot for him to come out from work. He finally walked out with his boss.

"What took you so long? Your mother and I have been waiting a long time."

His boss apologized and explained, "A coat was missing from our inventory, and we had to find it before I could let Michael leave."

Although I didn't say so, I had a feeling then that Mike had hidden the coat to steal it later.

During another instance, a car full of guys showed up at our house acting friendly.

"Hey Mike, come on and go with us." "Hey man, I can't go right now."

They all jumped out of the car shouting. I heard one of them holler, "You've got something of ours, and we want it NOW!"

They were going to beat Mike up right in our front yard.

I wasn't having that.

"Ya'll better get off our property", I yelled. "We're not going to have any fights here!"

Ignoring me, one of them threatened Mike as they jumped back into their car. "If we ever see you anywhere alone, we'll kill you!"

Mike was developing lots of enemies. I later heard that he had a big debt at a crack house. To pay off the debt, he may have taken all the things he stole from us and other people to that house, just like my father-in- law's Seiko watch, my class ring and Rhonda's leather coat.

Another episode was when I saw Michael steal money while he was working at my wife's leather booth in the mall. She and Mike were busy waiting on customers and stamping belts when I stopped by to visit them. Money had been missing. I suspected Mike was stealing, so I set him up.

"I'm going to the bathroom," I said. "Be back in a few minutes."

"Okay, Dad."

Actually, I went and sat around the corner and watched him sell something and pocket the money. He got pretty brave. Later I was standing near the booth when this guy walked up, bought something and gave Michael a twenty dollar bill. He rang it up, opened the drawer, pocketed the twenty, and gave the guy thirty cents in change. He closed the drawer and started laughing and talking to me as if nothing happened.

I said, "Mike, if you need some money for something, just asks me. Do not steal or take money from your Mama's business."

"What are you talking about, Dad?"

"I'm talking about that twenty dollar bill you just stuck in your pocket."

Michael got indignant and said, "I didn't put any money in my pocket."

"Well, turn around and let me stick my hand in your pocket and check. You don't mind my doing that, do you?"

Mike had the funniest look on his face. He stuck his hand in his pocket, pulled out the money and handed it to me.

I was just disgusted with him and said, "Mike, you eventually get caught when you do wrong."

CHAPTER 16

Michael had expensive tastes and always wanted more than we were able to provide. He continually fabricated stories to make us look wealthier than we were. He once told a group of guys our family didn't need to work. One of the fellows asked me what other kinds of businesses I owned. I told him I didn't own any businesses, but that my wife managed a leather business for a man from Mississippi.

I recall another incident that occurred in February of the year Michael died. He asked me to take him to the Cumberland County Courthouse.

"What for?" I asked.

"No bigdeal, Dad. I heard that the police want to ask me if I know anything about the break-ins in our neighborhood."

So, I carried him down there. As he hopped out of the truck, he said, "Just wait in the car, Dad. I won't be long."

Well, I waited and waited. He never came out, so I went into the courthouse to see if I could find him. As I walked by an office, a detective leaned out and said, "Hello, are you Michael Mobley's father?"

"Yes, I am," I said.

"Mr. Mobley, please come back here so we can talk," he said, motioning towards his office. "Your son has been arrested."

"Arrested? For what"? I asked.

"Well, Michael was involved in a break-in where an answering machine, some CDs and other things were stolen. We found an original tape in the answering machine and were able to trace it back to its owner. We then tied Mike to the break-in because his name was on the pawn ticket, and the pawn shop owner identified him."

I was speechless. I couldn't believe what I was hearing.

The detective continued, "Michael is currently being booked and finger printed, but we will release him into your custody rather than jail him. It's hard to believe he would be involved in a crime like this because he seems like such a nice young man. Mike told us that he couldn't remember anything about stealing the answering machine," the detective commented. "But he did remember that the driver of the car didn't have any identification, so Michael agreed to pawn the machine."

"Was Mike the only person involved?"

"No, but he wouldn't give us any other information."

I said, "Okay. I'll try to find out what's going on. Just send him out to the truck when you are finished."

"We will, but remember that he will have to appear in court.

If you can't afford a lawyer, the court will appoint you a public defender."

As I sat in the truck anxiously waiting, Mike nonchalantly walked down the courthouse steps, and then, seeing me, ditty-bopped across the parking lot with a wide grin and a pep-in-his-step-all's-right-with- his-world attitude.

As he opened the truck door and plopped down in the seat beside me, I said, "Well, Mike, did you get everything taken care of?"

"Oh yeah, no problem, I'm ready to go."

Pulling out of the parking lot I said, "What exactly did you have to take care of?" He went on to shoot me some kind of bull.

I reached over and grabbed his leg and said, "Mike, please tell me the truth. I know what's going on."

"What do you mean?" Michael asked with an innocent look on his face.

I said, "You took so long, I got out and went up to that door and spoke with the detective you were talking to. Now, do you want to tell me what's going on, or do you want me to tell you what's going on?"

"What did the detective tell you?" Michael asked. "He told me you were involved in breaking and entering someone's home and taking stuff that didn't belong to you, and pawning an answering machine."

"Yeah, you know, I don't remember doing any of that, but I am the one who pawned it."

"Who were the others involved?" "I can't tell you that, Dad."

"You mean to tell me you are going to go to court and take the rap for everybody else? You're going to take whatever they dish out? You're going to be totally responsible when I know you were not driving? Mike, the detective already told me that you weren't going to tell on your friends, but would take personal responsibility for whatever happened. The detective said, "That's loyal isn't it?" but I said, "No, that's stupidity! I was never so loyal to a friend that I would take the total rap for something they were involved in as well."

As we drove home, Mike had nothing else to say.

CHAPTER 17

M ike was finally indicted and a trial date was set, but it was postponed several times. We went to court on Tuesday, November 1, but it was three days before they called his case. On Thursday morning while we were waiting for the case to be called, the judge called a 30 minute recess.

Mike stood up and quietly said, "Padre, I'm going to the john."

"Okay. I'll wait here for you. Hurry back."

I waited and waited, but he didn't come back, so I got worried. Would he be late for his own trial? Would he be in contempt of court? Thank God, Mike showed up right before the break was over.

I asked him, "Where have you been?" "To the rest room."

"For thirty minutes?" He just shrugged it off.

It didn't dawn on me until later that Michael might have been down there praying, because he looked like he had been crying. He might have been praying that the judge would just let him go with a slap on the wrist or community service. Who knows.

That's basically what the judge did. They finally called his case, read the charges, and he pleaded guilty. The judge asked him to stand up and told Mike that he had seen him for the past three days. He commented that Mike was a clean cut looking guy, and said he was impressed with Michael wearing a suit. He suspended the prison sentence, reduced the charge from a felony to a misdemeanor, and then gave Mike a choice. He could accept probation for five years and perform community service work, or he could go to a boot camp that would teach him discipline. The judge gave Mike and me time to talk it over.

"Don't take the boot camp, Michael. Take the probation and community service. Even with five years, you can get off in two or three with good behavior. They will have a hearing every so often, and if they find out you are doing what you are supposed to, they may reduce your sentence.

"But Daddy, I can do this. I can handle the boot camp."

"Yeah, I know you lift weights and can handle it physically, but you know as well as I do, you can't get up on time for this boot camp."

"I still think I can do it, Dad."

"Mike, I know you think you can, but when you have these grand mal seizures, it's impossible to wake you up. (Mike's seizures were the result of past chemical use.)

"Son, I want you to take the probation."

After we talked about it, he turned around and walked back up beside his attorney, and said, "I've decided I'll take the boot camp."

I was floored! I couldn't believe what I heard.

The judge then gave me an opportunity to speak. I explained my concern about Mike's seizures affecting his ability to wake up in time to report.

Of course, the judge had to allow Mike to make the decision since he was of age.

Mike left his lawyer and walked back towards me. "Son, have you lost your mind?"

"Well, no. I think I can do it. I really think I can." "Well then, every morning when I wake you up, you'd better get up, because you have to be down there at 6:30 AM every morning, Monday through Friday. You have got to do it. One way or the other, you will be there."

"Okay, Dad."

As I drove Michael home, I replayed the events of the day in my mind. The judge seemed real impressed. Michael had the ability to charm people into believing anything. The judge told him that when he completed boot camp, the county would pay for his education at a technical school of Mike's choice. I thought the judge was more than lenient.

After his suicide, I started wondering whether or not his conviction is what pushed him over the edge. I think it really got to bearing on his mind that he couldn't follow through with the camp.

He knew he had to report to his probation officer Monday morning to get everything set up. The judge had told him that if he didn't report on Monday morning, they would come and arrest him. He then would be put in prison to serve his full time.

We can speculate forever, but we will never know the answer. Our son did not tell us why he took his life. I wonder if he had taken my advice, would he still be alive.

Now I feel cheated and devastated that he is gone. Mike was convicted on Thursday and dead on Sunday.

CHAPTER 18

The next time I saw my son he was lying in a casket. It looked like Michael from his eyes up. His face, nose and mouth had internal swelling from the suicide damage. The procurement company took a lot of skin and veins from him at the hospital. So the funeral home had to put his body in a plastic bag because the embalming fluid was leaking. His hair looked like Mike's, but not his face. I think they did the best they could with what they had to work with. There were a few bloodshot places on his face where some of the buckshot had come up near his skin.

Sometime after we got home from the funeral, I started thinking about how I had gotten closer to Mike in the past few months. In fact, I especially enjoyed the last Friday we spent together.

I remember that early that Friday Mike and I were getting the car aligned, and he was really anxious to call Rhonda at home. I told him to give her a call at the pay phone. I heard him say, "Rhonda, I am with Dad. Don't leave me. I'll be home soon."

She assured him she would wait for him. On that same afternoon Michael asked me about my friend Charlie who stuck a pistol in his mouth and pulled the trigger. His wife had left him and he'd been drinking at the time.

Michael asked me, "Dad, do you think Charlie went to heaven or hell since he took his own life?"

"I don't really know, Michael. I don't feel that Charlie was in his right state of mind. I think he went to heaven.

If I had thought about why Mike was asking, I may have put two and two together. I just thought he wanted to know about Charlie. It never even crossed my mind he was considering suicide.

Anyway, after we had that conversation, he was anxious to get home and go out with Rhonda. We got home about 5:30 or 6 PM. He and Rhonda left shortly to go visit all his friends. I guess he was saying goodbye. We never saw it coming. Even if he hadn't found a way to get that gun, I feel like he would have found some other way to commit suicide.

Why in the world would he do this? I know that we were good parents. We were always there to listen. All our children knew that whatever they were facing, they could come to us for help. Even their friends liked to come over and spend time with our family. They liked to eat dinner with us, spend the night, watch TV or just talk to us about their problems.

We were dead set against any kind of drugs, and all the kids knew that. Mike knew we would not approve of what he was doing. He became a master at hiding his double lifestyle.

CHAPTER 19

Mike's death caused a downhill ripple effect in our lives. We weren't mentally or physically able to make sound decisions. We tried to carry on our daily routine. I had been sick since 1981 and my condition worsened after the suicide. My wife had to work and make a living for both of us. Life was not the same. I couldn't deal with paying the bills, and didn't care whether they got paid or not. No matter what we did, there was no putting the joy back into our lives. We virtually tried to eat ourselves to death. I put on over a hundred pounds in 8 years, and Diane gained 150 pounds during that time. I had a heart attack in 1998, and Diane has had numerous health problems. So I guess the stress, anxiety, no rest and poor eating choices took their toll.

Eight years after Michael's death, my wife talked to me about writing this book. I couldn't believe it. Surely she wasn't serious! "Diane, what good do you think that is going to do now?" I asked. "Haven't we been through enough? Why do you want to stir up the hurt and pain that we've already suffered?"

She explained that she wasn't trying to cause more pain in our lives, but she was trying to help others. I admired Diane's courage. The longer she worked on the book, the more I noticed changes in her. She finally began to look and acts like the Diane I fell in love with. She could talk about our son without crying. No longer did my wife bury his memory, but her writing helped us both to make Michael a part of our lives again.

Diane

In 2008 Ronnie's health failed fast. Ronnie developed pulmonary fibrosis after having pneumonia 12 times. All of Ronnie's illnesses were complications from the rheumatoid arthritis. In addition I had problems walking. Osteoarthritis made my job almost impossible.

Kelly, our oldest daughter, and her husband Pete invited us to live with them in Michigan. Von and I stopped working on the book when we moved. We worked for 6 years but still didn't finish. Ronnie and I lived in Michigan for 6 months before he died. He loved Michigan every minute we were there. After he passed away in 2008, it took three more years before I was able to finish the book.

CHAPTER 20

Ye lived in painful darkness, like being in the pits of hell.
I think that's the reason we were so concerned about
Rhonda after Michael passed away. We didn't want to be too strict
on her, because we didn't want to lose another child. We weren't
making very good decisions at that time and neither was Rhonda.

One week Rhonda went with me to a counseling session.
While I was talking to the counselor, Rhonda just broke down
sobbing. I took her in my arms to comfort her. That's when she
confessed that Michael talked to her about suicide the night before
he died. She felt guilty for not telling us. I let her know right away
she had nothing to feel guilty about, that none of us knew what
Michael was thinking. This is when Rhonda decided to tell her
story.

Rhonda

After eight years my Mama asked me to help her remember
what happened to Michael. I thought, "Unbelievable! All these
years later she wants me to resurrect everything I have tried to
forget?" She explained that she wanted to help two groups of
people, the ones who consider suicide and the loved ones left with
the excruciating pain.

I looked at her like she was crazy. "No way," I said.

Mama said, "Rhonda, I need your help and talking will help us deal with the pain." I couldn't believe we were having this conversation. I got really mad so I immediately left her house before I blew up. By the time I got home I was hysterical.

It was months before I was able to sit down with Mama and talk about my brother.

During those months I continually asked myself, "Why? Why did he do it?" I know my brother was scared of going to jail. He knew he wouldn't stand a chance in prison because he was such a pretty boy. Michael was discouraged, frustrated, in pain and felt like a failure. He knew that he had disappointed everyone. My brother just couldn't get his life right. He saw no way out. Everything piled up on him until he just snapped.

CHAPTER 21

M y relationship with my brother completely changed during the last year of his life. I do not remember as much as I would like to about Michael, but I do know that for the first time, I really liked him.

We grew up as other children did, arguing, fighting, and having differences, but Michael finally started acting like my friend instead of beating me up.

A few weeks before he killed himself, he really surprised me. Some of his friends were hanging out at our house. I was in the living room and heard them open the front door to leave. As they were heading out, I heard Michael say, "Hold on just a second, guys." Then he turned around and ran back to find me.

He gave me a hug and said, "I love you. I'll see you later." I thought to myself, "that was weird" since he had never hugged or kissed me before, but I really liked it.

That last year, Michael and I hung out together a lot. Daddy had taken his license away, so I was his main means of transportation. Michael made a bunch of wrong decisions---drugs, witchcraft, stealing and lying. It just got to the point that he didn't know what to do. A lot of his friends weren't hanging out with him anymore because of the way the drugs were affecting his mind. The acid and other drugs caused him to have seizures and flashbacks

My family and I were never quite sure what kinds of drugs he used or what lies he was telling, but one thing we did know. Friends and other people were talking. Michael was unable to keep his drug use a secret anymore. His life was unraveling. He was becoming more and more depressed each day.

He started going back to church to try to make things better. On the surface he appeared to be doing well. Like a chameleon, he would instantaneously change his personality to suit the situation at any given moment. My brother knew how to fit in with any lifestyle---from Christians to drug dealers.

CHAPTER 22

The week before Michael died was a typical week for me. I was going to school and hanging out with my friends. Michael and I made plans to go out Friday night. Late Friday afternoon he called me from a pay phone and said, "Don't leave me, Rhonda. Dad and I are on our way home."

When we left that night, we stopped by to see one of Michael's friends. The guy said his wife would be home soon, so we didn't stay long. From what I can remember, Michael got a bag of weed from him. We left and rode around Cross Creek Mall for a while. He decided he was ready to go to Daniel's to spend the night.

On the way we stopped to get Michael a cheeseburger at P.D. Quick. It was taking a long time at the drive-thru, so Michael was hollering out, "Hurry up, people, I'm starving!!!" The girl came to the window and said, "I am so sorry for the wait. We had to cook it fresh since it is so late." She was a girl I went to school with. I turned and spit out, "Michael, shut up, you are embarrassing me." I noticed he had a crazy look in his eyes. I thought to myself, *you are strange Michael Mobley.*

As we continued to wait for his food, I recalled that once when I had touched him he turned and glared at me, and with a threatening voice I didn't even recognize, said, "Get your hands off me!" That really scared me. I thought to myself, but this is why I wanted Daddy to put a lock on my bedroom door. Some nights when I would wake up, he'd be standing over my bed staring at me. Was he having a seizure? Walking in his sleep? Going to steal some more of my stuff? Either way, I was becoming more and more afraid for my brother.

After we finally got his food and were on the way to Daniel's house, he asked me, "Do you think people who commit suicide still go to heaven?"

"I don't know, Michael," I said, and thought nothing else about him saying it. Not until he killed himself. Then his comment ate away at me for the next eight years. It took that long for me to tell Mama that he had asked that question the night before he died.

Saturday night I went to bed around midnight. Shortly after that Daddy left to go pick up Michael from Daniel's. I knew my brother was in trouble for not coming home earlier, and being a nosey 17-year-old, I left my door open so I could hear everything my parents were going to say. I just couldn't wait to tease my brother the next day.

A few minutes later in they came. Daddy and Mike were arguing about Mike not calling or coming home on time. My Mom was getting dressed to go to work. She overheard them and jumped in to explain to Daddy that she had cut the phone off to get some rest. They talked a little longer and then I heard my brother's voice from the hallway saying, "You won't have to worry about me anymore."

Even though things got quiet, they all were still uptight. I could feel it. I was still lying on my bed in the dark, pretending to be asleep and waiting to hear what else might be said. Sometime after that Mama must have told Michael that she loved him, because I heard him say, "I love you too, Mama."

In a few minutes I heard the front door close. I knew everything was going to be okay, so I relaxed and was drifting off to sleep when Michael came into my room.

"Rhonda, you got any cigarettes? Can I have one?" "Yeah, they're on my dresser."

I went peacefully to sleep only to wake up hours later, to loud screeching sounds. It sounded like Mom laughing hysterically. I couldn't believe all that noise while I was trying to sleep, so I hollered out, "Ya'll shut up!" All of the sudden my Dad slowly pushed my door open and turned on the light. I immediately saw he was crying and his face was deathly white.

"Rhonda, Michael's dead."

"Whaaaaaat? Michael's dead? Oh, my God, no," I screamed as I jumped out of bed. I rushed across the hall to my brother's room and noticed my mama at the end of the hall talking to someone on the phone.

I stepped through the door and saw Michael on his bed with his pillow over his face. I first thought, no, he's okay; he's just done some bad drugs. Then I lifted the pillow and saw the hole in his chin. I knew he was dead. Instantly it crushed me. I just couldn't believe that my brother was dead. This could not be happening! Blood had puddled under Michael on his mattress and had run down on the floor. Daddy cautioned me not to touch him or the gun that lay between his legs. All I could do was scream, "Noooooooooooooo!"

My legs became weak. My body collapsed to the floor. Daddy went down with me. He held me in his arms. Mom rushed to us and we all huddled in the hallway, crying and screaming. It was Sunday morning, November 6, 1994. Our family's nightmare had just begun.

CHAPTER 23

It seemed like it took the police days to get to our house. Everything was crazy. I felt sick. I was mad and everyone else was to blame. I don't recall thinking about how my mom and dad were feeling. I was only thinking about how much I was hurting inside.

Finally the police arrived. They came into Michael's room and asked me to leave. I did not want to leave, but I did as they asked even though it really made me mad. I went to my room and found a picture of Michael. I remember just staring at it and crying because I could not believe that my brother was dead. One of the police officers asked me to go to the porch and sit with my mother so that I would be out of the house. The officer had to help me up from the floor because my legs were so weak.

I asked the officer if I could take the picture with me and he said, "Yes that will be fine."

I walked out of my bedroom, as the police snapped pictures in Michael's room. Officers filled our kitchen. They talked and laughed as if nothing had happened. I thought "How dare you!" I wanted to scream, "HEY! Stop talking! Wake him up! Aren't police officers supposed to be heroes? Why can't you bring him back?" I was livid and I resented every one of them being in my house. If they couldn't fix it, they needed to leave.

I stepped out on the porch, and watched an officer wrap yellow tape around the pine trees in our front yard. I sat down with my mama on the bench Daddy had made. We watched the cars pass by and slow down while the people stared at us. I was wondering what they were thinking since yellow tape usually meant a crime scene.

My nerves were shot. I had to have a cigarette. I asked one of the officers if I could go back in the house and get my pack. He replied, "No."

"Either you are going to go get my cigarettes or I am going to get them myself! Now you decide!"

I don't know if it was my tone of voice, my red hair, my red face, or a combination of the three, but the officer then asked, "Well, where are your cigarettes?"

"They are in my brother's room on his table beside his bed," I snapped back.

To keep the peace, he went in and brought me my cigarettes. I lit up and took a deep draw, two paramedics pulled into the driveway in an emergency vehicle. Immediately Mom turned to me and said, "Let's go into the den and get out of the way."

We finally noticed a well-dressed man in a black suit who had followed us into our den. Who was he? Why was he here? What was he going to say? He sat down in the chair next to our back door and began to explain why people commit suicide. He read a few Bible verses to us while we sat there staring at him. He was trying to make us feel better only to upset us worse. I felt like slapping him. I thought, "Mama if you don't stop this man from talking, I am going to have to take matters into my own hands!" Thank God. He finally shut up!

CHAPTER 24

M ama decided that it was time to get me out of the house and away from all the confusion. Neither of us needed to see Michael's body leaving our house in a plastic bag. Mama said, "We need to go tell your Grandma and Kelly right now before they hear it somewhere else."

I asked a police officer to remove the yellow tape so that we could get out of the yard. As I drove down the road it seemed like the trip would never end. Mama sobbed and stared out the window. It was so horrible for her.

I heard more sirens and then saw rescue vehicles coming over the hill headed in the direction of our home. I asked Mama, "Do you think they are going to our house? Exactly how many paramedics and police does it take for one person?" Mama said, "I don't know Rhonda." She continued to stare out the window for the next ten miles until we finally pulled into Grandma's driveway.

After telling Grandma what had happened, the phone rang. I picked it up and said, "Hyman's residence," just like I always do. The person on the other end was crying so hard I could barely understand what he was saying. He finally calmed down and said, "This is Bryan." I wondered how he already knew about Michael. He continued, "Rhonda, I am so sorry. What happened?"

"Michael killed himself!" I screeched. I was furious with Bryan for not being there when Michael needed him. He and my brother had been very close, but Bryan had disowned Michael months before. Still, Bryan was crying, so I told him, "It's okay." That was all I knew to say. We soon hung up.

Later, I went out and sat on Grandma's porch swing, watching family and friends come and go. I was laughing because it was the only way I knew how to handle the situation. People looked at me like I was crazy, but I just couldn't help it. Many friends came up and hugged my neck, offering lots of well-meaning comments and advice. As I smiled back at them I was thinking, "What do you know? I am the one going through this, not you."

The next day Mama and Daddy had to make funeral arrangements. As if it wasn't already difficult enough, they now had to decide where to bury Michael and how in the world they would pay for it.

The nightmare continued at the wake. It was awful. Some people were staring at us and talking. A few of Michael's friends walked up and asked me if we were going to open the casket. I said I didn't think so but I would ask. My parents and the funeral director agreed to open it for a short time.

I was one of the first to walk up with my childhood friend, Ronette. I almost fell to the floor when I looked at him. Michael didn't look like himself. He face was swollen. I could not believe I was at Michael's funeral. I never expected to see my brother dead in a casket. Ronette and I both went crazy. Both my mom and hers came running wrapped their arms around us and pulled us away toward a couch where they held us and tried to comfort us.

The funeral was the same. More torment-more tragedy. When they lowered my brother into the ground, his body was not the only thing buried that day. I buried my feelings about his suicide and all my memories of Michael.

On Monday morning after the funeral, I went back to school. As I walked into the bathroom, I saw a friend and she said, "Rhonda, I saw you and your friend this morning in the office and you were talking about me."

"I don't know what you are talking about. I just lost my brother," I replied.

She grabbed my long pony tail and pulled me down and started to beat me in the face and stomach. I could not get away from her. Someone grabbed me from the back and held my arms. I used my elbows to hit the person behind so I could get loose and protect myself. A teacher came in and pulled that girl off me. That was when I realized that I was elbowing a teacher and not another student. They took us to the office. I tried to explain what happened, but the principal would not listen. We were both suspended for three days.

When Daddy and I went back after the third day, the principal informed us that I would be suspended for two weeks. That really upset me because I knew right away, I would fail my grade. My Daddy was wonderful to me that day. He turned to me, gave me a hug and said, "Rhonda, it will be okay, Baby." I knew my Daddy was mad, but very calmly said to my principal, "You will not have to worry about Rhonda." My wife and I discussed this with Rhonda for the past three days. We all agree it will be best for her if we make other arrangements for her education. Rhonda has been through more than even an adult could handle. Enough is enough.

When I left school that day, it was the end of my youth. I left behind my friends, my prom and my high school graduation. I later got my GED from a community college, but I felted cheated. It was just one more thing that I blamed on my brother.

"I'm so angry with you, Michael Todd Mobley."

CHAPTER 25

If only I could talk to Michael or write him a letter. These are some of the things I would say:

"What did we ever do to you, Michael Mobley? That's all I want to know. Why did you want us to hurt for the rest of our lives? What did you think we would do? Walk in there and clap and jump up and down? Celebrate? Cheer with each other? Yeah! He's gone! Oh boy! Let's have a party! He's killed himself and we don't have to worry about him anymore. That's what your note said.

Is that what you thought? Did you want us to hurt for the rest of our lives? Why did you do it? Like you thought we weren't going to find you? I mean that's what I want to know, Michael. I know you left a note saying you were sorry for all the pain you caused. Why would you do it in the house where your mama and daddy are going to find you? Did you want all of us to live with that pain for the rest of our lives? Michael, you were only thinking of yourself."

Michael's suicide nearly made me lose my mind. It really did. I didn't understand a lot of things. I just didn't understand. I could not understand how it happened and why it happened or what went wrong. I was only sixteen years old. My brother's death ruined my life and crushed my childhood dreams of becoming a model or a dancer. His suicide is the most devastating thing that's happened in my life. Michael's death tore out a piece of my heart.

Michael left a note saying he didn't want to hurt us anymore. By making that decision, he ended up hurting all of us more than he could ever know.

I think that he had plotted and planned for a long time how he was going to do it without us realizing what was in his mind. Some people say it takes a lot of guts to commit suicide. But I think it takes a coward to make that decision, someone who is scared to live and work out their problems.

I don't know why he did it. I just don't know. Did Michael believe that we would be better off without him? Michael probably told himself, "If you kill yourself they won't worry about you anymore, and you won't go to prison." Was suicide the only way that he thought he could get out of his situation? I don't know. But that's what he did. When will it all end?

To this day, many mornings before I open my eyes, I say to myself, "Open your eyes, Rhonda, you're going to be back in your bedroom. Mama and Daddy will be home soon. You and Michael can go somewhere and do something. You have just had a bad dream. Now open your eyes, Rhonda, and Michael will be here." But every morning, I wake up and my life still continues without my brother. That's just the way it is.

I'm very proud of my daughters. Rhonda has grown up to be a wonderful daughter, wife, and mother of two great kids. In February, 2011, she was diagnosed with multiple sclerosis. She has a strong spirit and works hard to improve her health.

Kelly is doing great. She is married and has three wonderful kids.

One thing that Kelly said to me after Michael died was that I was a good mother. Thank you, Kelly, for having faith in me.

CHAPTER 26

Abi's Story as told to Michael's mother on September 20, 2002

I was 12 or 13 when I first met Michael in 1992 at Ft. Caswell (Baptist Retreat Center on the NC coast). I had on an outfit with sheer sleeves, and I wore my hair up in a ponytail most of the time. I remember him because he picked on me about looking like that woman on the TV show, "I Dream of Jeannie." I remember I wanted to be cool back then and smoke cigarettes like some of the kids at church, but Michael would always get on me. "You don't need to smoke cigarettes," he would say.

"You're too young. It makes you look ugly."

We were fond of each other, but there was such an age difference that we just talked on the phone a lot. I was going through some stressful times, so he just encouraged me. He never tried to push himself on me or do anything wrong.

During the summer of 1994 we were celebrating our last night at Ft. Caswell. We decided to dress alike during the last service.

I had saved a sundress all week that had burgundy flowers that matched the burgundy in his vest. Some of the girls had fixed my hair for me. It was one of my favorite nights, because Michael was really sweet. I was so happy that night.

One night during that last week at Caswell, Michael had one of his dreams (seizures) where he got up in the middle of the night and walked through the house screaming. The noise woke up several people. I ran and got our church leader. That's the first time Michael talked to me about doing drugs. He would have flashbacks in his dreams and get up to act them out. I felt close to him then because he confided in me. Usually it was me talking to him about my problems.

I had no idea, no clue about his drug use. Someone had told me earlier that Michael had a drug problem, but I just didn't believe it. I just blew it off. That's why I had so many questions after he killed himself. I just didn't understand. I knew I didn't cause it, but I just kept asking, "Why? Why in the world?" At that time, I didn't know he was going to court or that he had any charges against him. I kept asking my friends in the youth group, "Whose fault is this?" Nobody had the answers I needed, so I just left the church.

When I went to church Sunday morning, November 6, I found out Michael had killed himself. I fell to the floor. His death made me question my religion and a lot about my life. I walked out of the church and had a friend take me over to my mother's house in St. Paul's. I never went back to the church for the next two years.

The day after Michael died I moved out from my grandparent's home and in with my mama. I went from "straight A's," attending church every Sunday, and being involved in community activities, to running the roads. I never did buy drugs, but I spent a lot of money, part of my college fund, on clothes and other stuff teenage girls want.

During my wild years from 1994-96, many people offered me acid. I knew I wasn't going to try it because of what it had done to Michael. It scared me so bad. I always thought it would be my luck to get that bad trip. I have thought all these years that Michael's death was because of a flash back from acid or some other drug. I thought he didn't know what he was doing, couldn't stand it, and killed himself.

I got pregnant at age 16. Two years to the very day Michael died, I had my daughter Olivia. My due date was November 19, but she was born three weeks premature. The doctors told me that they might have to give me a C-section. I told them there was no need. Remembering the 6th was the anniversary of Michael's death, I knew I was going to have her that day. My daughter was born at 10:28 PM.

That's when I decided to go back and finish school. Because of Olivia I needed to turn my life around. Having my daughter was healing for me.

I can't explain it, but I believe that Michael had a part in it. Had Olivia been a boy, I probably would have named him Michael.

There is nothing bad anybody could say to me about Michael, because he was just too kindhearted. I understand he did bad things and hung with the wrong crowd, but that didn't make Michael a bad person. He wanted everyone to think well of him. He always thought he could handle anything.

(*After hearing about Michael's conviction and court sentence, Abi continues.*)

I think he didn't want to face the fact that he was sick. I don't think Michael's death was due to anyone else's influence. I believe he was battling a lot of things. He couldn't see how everything could work out. He probably thought your family would get over his death eventually, and go on about your lives. Michael didn't know it was a pain that would last forever.

When a friend as close as Michael kills himself, it shows you suicide is permanent. It is forever. There is no going back. There's no taking it back.

There is nothing you can do once you've pulled that trigger. I have never attempted suicide, but I think it crosses every teenager's mind at some point. When you have seen suicide up close, you realize it cannot be an option.

CHAPTER 27

Kaye

What a difference the years of drugs can make in a wonderful person's life.

Unfortunately, my last memory of Michael was in October 1993 when my Dad died. That was approximately one year prior to Michael's suicide.

I was on my way home from a vacation in Hawaii when I received the phone call that my Dad had passed away. I made arrangements for my now adult kids, John and Jamie, to meet me in Los Angeles for the flight to North Carolina to be with my Mom and to attend the funeral.

Over the past years, my sister, Diane, had shared many of the worries, the concerns, and the results that drugs had made on Michael's life.

There were sporadic changes in his personality. The seizures and nightmares would erupt leaving him with no memory of the events. He stole to support his habit. Bottom line, we all were worried about him.

When we arrived in Fayetteville, it was wonderful to see my family, even under the sad circumstances of my Dad's death.

The day of the funeral Michael, wanting to spend as much time possible with family and with his cousins John and Jamie, asked if he could spend the night.

We were all elated that he wanted to be at Granny's with us. All seemed well with Michael that day…at least, so far.

Sometime during the night, we all were awakened with a loud noise coming from the bedroom where Michael was asleep. My son, John, was the first one in the room to observe Michael having a nightmare or hallucinations.

Needless to say, we were all unnerved by this event, and very worried about Michael. Granny was able to calm him down and get him back to bed that night. The following day, he was once again the Michael we all knew and loved, with no memory of the previous night's event.

When I returned home to California, my thoughts often travelled to that night and to the hope and prayer that Michael would be able to fight the drugs that had overtaken his body. Sadly, his drug use changed him from a bright-eyed young man with many hopes and dreams to become an astronaut, to a young man that many of us often no longer recognized. He was certainly intelligent enough to turn his astronaut dream into a reality.

CHAPTER 28

Suicide is so much more than just your loved one dying. It's the living that's the killer. One day at a time, I deal with the guilt, the blame, the shame, the anger and the failure.

We are all suffering and we have lost faith in our own judgment. I thought I was a good mother, but now I feel like I failed. I failed Michael and now I'm probably failing Rhonda. My life is shattered into little pieces. Each day I get up and decide what piece of my life can I pick up today?

From the time Michael died my personality completely changed. I didn't want to be around people or for them to talk to me. I am extremely angry, defensive, bitter, sad and hurt.

Before Michael died I thought the best of people, but afterwards my reality was distorted. I didn't trust anybody. I didn't even trust my own judgment because I thought my son was doing well.

At first we all blamed ourselves for Michael's death. Somebody had to be at fault. Then we blamed some of Michael's friends, each other, and anybody else who came to mind. We looked at this from every angle to see if we caused his suicide, or did something to push him over the edge. But I can't help but go back to the fact that we now know that he was planning this for months. My son was just waiting for the right opportunity. I now realize we will never know why, on this particular night, Michael decided to die.

CHAPTER 29

Ronnie and I left the last of January to go on a trip. Before leaving I fixed a basket of 24 long stemmed silk red roses for Valentine's Day and put on Michael's grave. After we returned, Mother and I went by the grave site. As we pulled around the corner, we could see in the distance that the flowers were gone. I pulled up beside Daddy's and Michael's graves and parked. As we sat in the car we both were softly crying. Not wanting to upset Mom any more than she was, I pulled away from the curb and left.

I decided that day that I would buy dollar flowers so they wouldn't be stolen. But, no matter what I did the flowers were always gone. That hurt so badly that I decided not to put any more flowers on his grave. I have people ask me, "Where are Michael's flowers? His grave looks as if no one cares about him." After I explain why I buy flowers and keep them in the house in honor of Michael, they seem to understand.

Until you decide to deal with the pain, it sits inside of you like a cancer and devours your soul. It paralyzes you to the point that your life is not worth living.

CHAPTER 30

2012

I first decided to write this book in the summer of 2002. I asked a longtime friend, Von, to help me with the typing and spelling. Von was a blessing to me. Without her help I could not have finished the book at all.

When we first started writing, I did a lot of preliminary work at home. We would work at Von's home once a week for two hours. Sometimes I could work the whole time, but other times it would make me sick to my stomach. I would say, "Sorry Von, I can't do anymore today." I didn't know until we quit working together that it made Von sick, too. What a dedicated friend who put aside time to help me find my joy and peace again.

When we were working on the book, each week would get a little easier. I took one step forward and two backwards. It hurt so bad to talk about Michael and his suicide. But the reward was greater than the pain as I continued pushing forward. It was more than enough to make it all worthwhile. Little by little I was getting better. I could talk with my family and friends about Michael.

Now I love being around people again and I have my joy and peace back.

A big plus is I've lost 110 lbs. The shame of losing Michael caused me to overeat. I thought it was my fault. I used food to comfort me. If I hurt, I ate. If I got emotionally upset, I ate. At night I would read or watched T.V. and ate. Smoking and drinking was not an option for me, but eating was acceptable in the Church. Eating didn't fill the emptiness that losing Michael had left in my heart. Making Michael a part of my life again and writing this book did.

We can't do anything about the past, but going forward we can choose how we live our life. I choose to live my life more abundantly.

CHAPTER 31

Without the pain of losing our son, we would have missed the joy of this little boy and young man named Michael Todd Mobley.

Talking about the story of Michael's life and death has turned some hopeless people's lives around. They have decided to live.

This is all I had hoped and prayed for—that all our pain and suffering would not be in vain – that this book would be a turning point for young and old, people hurt by suicide or contemplating suicide. All I ask is that you give life another chance.

Michael didn't live long enough to achieve personal greatness, but through his death, his story will bring help and healing to people who have been affected by suicide. Michael's story was his destiny and my writing his story is mine.

The Face of Suicide

Michael Todd Mobley

Do you have a loved one or friend who has talked about suicide, who is depressed, who has withdrawn from friends and activities, who has a sense of hopelessness?

Don't wait until it's too late to get them help.
1-800-SUICIDE
1-800-999-9999

www.ingramcontent.com/pod-product-compliance
Lightning Source LLC
Chambersburg PA
CBHW071530120626
46550CB00006B/2408